Dandaofa Xuan

單刀法選

THE JAPANESE PIRATE SWORD

Published 1614

Cheng Zongyou 程宗猷

Translated by Eric Shahan

単刀法選
The Japanese Pirate Sword
Translator's Introduction

Painting showing Ming Era Chinese soldiers on the left fending off Wakou pirates on the right.

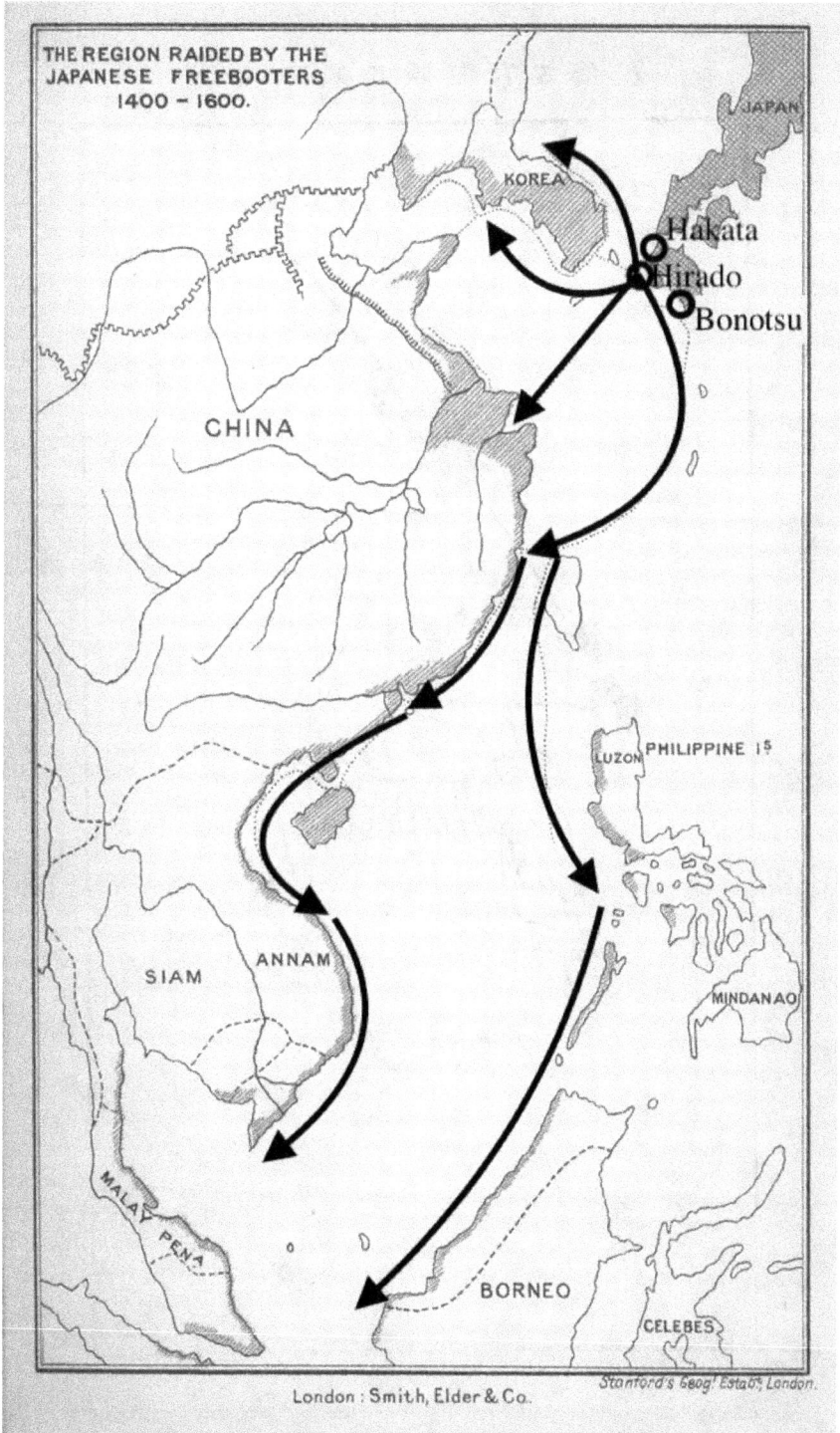

THE REGION RAIDED BY THE
JAPANESE FREEBOOTERS
1400 – 1600.

JAPAN

KOREA

Hakata
Hirado
Bonotsu

CHINA

LUZON   PHILIPPINE IS

SIAM   ANNAM

MINDANAO

MALAY PEN^A

BORNEO

CELEBES

London : Smith, Elder & Co.

Stanford's Geog.l Estab.t London.

明人の眼に映じたる倭寇

Translator's Introduction
Wakou Japanese Pirates

From the mid-1300s to the mid-1500s, Wakou, Japanese Pirates, raided the southeastern coast of China. Wakou 倭寇, is comprised of two Kanji. The first, Wa 倭 is the oldest word used to describe Japan, and means "submissive, distant, dwarf." It was used in reference to the inhabitants of the Kingdoms in Kyushu as well as the Yamato Kingdom from the 3ʳᵈ century until about 800 AD. Later, the Japanese replaced it with another Kanji, also read as Wa, but meaning "harmony and peace." The second Kanji, Kou 寇 means "pirate or foreign invader."

The Wakou attacks peaked in a period known as 嘉靖大倭寇 *The Great Japanese Pirate Attacks of the Jiajing Period*, roughly from 1522 to 1566 A.D. During this period China was dealing with two military situations: raids by Mongols from the north and Wakou pirates along the southeastern coast. This problem was known as 北虜南倭 *Japanese attacking in the South, Mongols attacking in the North*.

Wakou, while not particularly good at naval fighting, were expert swordsmen and archers. They were armed with long, thin, single edged swords held in two hands. This contrasted with the short, one-handed swords used by the Chinese soldiers. Further, many Wakou pirates fought nearly naked, with only a loin cloth.[1] Their tactics sewed confusion as well. When they faced off against opponents, they used mocking stances, taunting their opponents before delivering a single, great killing blow. Their swords and tactics. became greatly feared.

However enraging their tactics, the Chinese were initially at a loss as to how to defend against the Katana wielding pirates. Eventually, the Chinese forces captured a scroll showing the Kenjutsu, or sword fighting techniques, used by the pirates and began to learn how they fought. The captured scroll, though incomplete, was deemed so valuable it was reprinted in a Chinese military manual in 1561.

---

[1] The text on top of the picture on the previous page says, "How people of the Ming Era viewed the Wakou pirates."

Kage School Catalogue found in		
New Treatise on Military Efficiency 紀效新書 1561		
Description Part 3	Description Part 2	Description Part 1
Stance 2		Stance 1
Stance 4		Stance 3

The Techniques

The scroll, from the Kage "Shadow" School of Sword, was captured from pirates in the mid-16th century. It contains a list of techniques and a few brief descriptions before ending abruptly. The Kage School was founded Aisu Ikosai (1452 ~ 1538) and is considered one of the Three Great Founding Schools of Sword Fighting, along with the Nen School and the Shinto School. The scroll, titled *A Catalogue of Shadow School Techniques* was published in volume 4 of *New Treatise on Military Efficiency* 紀效新書. The author is known as Seki Keiko 戚継光 in Japan and Qi Jiguang in China.

Kage Ryu Catalogue

Enpi/ Flying Monkey
This technique has a strong relationship to any opening the opponent may give and your Tachi.
Totobi/Flying Tiger
Seigan/Clear Shore
Kagemi/ Seen From the Shadow

Further, do not allow your sword to get in sync with the opponent's Tachi. No matter how difficult your opponent do not change the position of the tip of your sword. This is an extremely important point. This (way of fighting) is known as Kokiri, or cutting off the corners. Indeed you should follow the way of cutting described in this method.

Enkai/ Circling Monkey

This technique is for when you are facing many opponents. You should not allow your Tachi to sync with the enemy's Tachi. Seize the time that is to your advantage. Your mind should be as it was when you were at the Shodan, or low level, of swordsmanship.

Third: Yamakage/ Shadow of the Mountain
(Scroll ends here)

◎日本刀

島夷出沒如飛集、　右手持刀左持盾、　大舶輕艘海上行、　華人未見心先阻、

千金重募來殺賊、　賊退心驕酬不得、　爾財吾豪婦吾家、　省命防城誰敢責。

（島夷行）

死を見る歸するが如し、跳梁蝶の若しと所有驚嘆の修辭を以て描かれし倭寇の

武器について、彼れまた誌して曰く

太刀

一、太刀

長サ五尺餘、雙刀ヲ用キレハ丈餘地ニ及ヒ、又手ヲ加ヘテ舞フ。鋒ヲ開ケハ凡

ソ八尺、舞動スレハ則チ上下四旁悉ク白ウシテ其ノ人ヲ見ス。

竹弓

二、竹弓

長サ八尺、足ヲ以テ弰ヲ踏ミ立チナガラ矢ヲ發ス。矢ハ海蘆ヲ以テ幹トナシ、

鐵ヲ以テ鏃トナス。鏃ノ廣サ二寸、燕尾ヲナシ重サ二三兩、人ニ近付イテ發ス、

中ラザルナシ。

又曰ク

中レバ則チ立所ニ倒ル。

xii

Other References to the Weapons Used by Wakou Pirates

Nihonto The Japanese Sword

They come flying out from the barbarian islands like falcons
In their right hand they carry the Katana, in their left, a shield.
They travel the seas in great fleets of ships
Chinese have never seen people with this spirit
They repeatedly steal from us and kill
We allow these thieves to be rewarded
The mean to steal our valuables and stuff them in a sack with our
wives, Who is to blame for not saving us and defending the cities?

From 島夷行 *Visitors From the Barbarian Islands*
Date and author unknown.

Tachi : Longsword

Each pirate uses two swords with blades that are 5 Shaku, 150 centimeters. They move back and forth across a wide area and when they use their hands it is as if they are dancing. Once they knock your spearpoint aside they move in 8 Shaku, 240 centimeters, either up, down, left right and any other direction so it is as if they have become colorless and you can no longer see them.

Takeyumi : Bamboo Bow

Their bows are 8 Shaku, 240 centimeters, tall and they stand the bottom nock on the ground when shooting arrows. The body of the arrows are made of Ashi, a kind of reed, and the points are forged iron. The arrowheads are about 2 Sun, 6 cm, in diameter and shaped like a swallow's tail. If two or three people approach, they will fire and not miss. Anyone struck by one of these arrows will fall.

Further, it is also said that the southwestern island of Japan is called Devil's Island. That is where they produce iron. The local inhabitants enjoy fighting and thus the Japanese recruit pirates from there. There are both white devils and black devils.

白鬼黑鬼

倭國ノ西南ニ鬼國アリ利鐵ヲ產ス。士人爭鬪ヲ好ミ,倭ノ寇スルヤ多ク其ノ

族ヲ慕ル。白鬼黑鬼アリ。

三、銃

銅ヲ以テ鑄成シ,利錐ニテ穴ヲ鑿チ,光潤木柄ヲ用ヰズ,特ニ緊シテ裝彈シ,從ウ

テ發スレバ從ウテ至リ,聲ナク避クルモ及バズ。

Ju
Gun

They melt metal and pour it into a mold. Then they drill a hole into it. They don't attach a lacquered wood handle. The pirates grip it in their elbow to load. Once they fire the sound is such that you will flee without uttering a sound.

Longsword, Bamboo Bow and *Gun* from *The Bubishi*
Mao Yuanyi
Published in 1621

武器䂖図

An Illustrated Guide to 200 Weapons
by Kobyayashi Sukemichi 小林 祐猷
Published in 1848.

It is not clear what kind of sword the Wakou pirates used, but clearly it is very long. *An Illustrated Guide to 200 Weapons* shows several long swords. The Nodachi "field sword" as well as the Naga Tachi "long sword" are good candidates.

	Present Day R: Wakizashi Short Sword L: Chisa Katana Small Sword .		R: Nodachi Field Sword L: Thread Wrapped Tachi .
	R: Tiger Fur Scabbard Cover L: Bear Fur Scabbard Cover .		R: Hyogo Gusari Tachi Hyogo Region Chain Tachi L: Naga Tachi Long Sword .
	Top : Fire Starting Kit Center: Scabbard Cover Lower: Hip Protector .		R: Shirogane Zukuri Tachi Tachi With Silver Fittings L: Kuro Tachi Black Side Katana .
	R: Hairpin C: Small Knife L: Piercing Knife		R: Uchidachi Striking Katana C:Koshi Gatana Waist Katana L: Metezasi Utility Knife

Song of the Japanese Sword 日本刀歌
Ouyang Xiu 欧陽修 (1007 ~ 1072)

昆夷道遠不復通，世傳切玉誰能窮

寶刀近出日本國，越賈得之滄海東

魚皮裝貼香木鞘，黃白閒雜鍮與銅

百金傳入好事手，佩服可以禳妖凶

傳聞其國居大島，土壤沃饒風俗好

其先徐福詐秦民，採藥淹留丱童老

百工五種與之居，至今器玩皆精巧

前朝貢獻屢往來，士人往往工詞藻

徐福行時書未焚，逸書百篇今尚存

令嚴不許傳中國，舉世無人識古文

先王大典藏夷貊，蒼波浩蕩無通津

令人感激坐流涕，繡澀短刀何足云

The Japanese Sword

From the 10th century onward Japanese swords as well as the scabbards and fittings had a reputation as high quality in China. In fact dozens of poets created works titled *Song of the Japanese Sword, starting with the* poet Ouyang Xiu (1007 ~ 1072.)

Song of the Japanese Sword 日本刀歌
by Ouyang Xiu

The region where "Western Warlike People" live is far and hard to reach. It is said they make swords so sharp they can cut through jade as if it were made of earth, but no one alive can say they have seen them. Recently, the most marvelous swords have come to us from Japan. A Yue merchant acquired them from the after crossing the blue sea to the east. The scabbards are made from a fragrant wood, and sharkskin is attached to them. The fittings are a mixture of brass, nickel and copper.

The blades are bought for a hundred pieces of gold by those who fancy them. When worn they protect the bearer from evil spirits. They originate from a great island country that has fertile lands and people with good customs and traditions.

Long ago the alchemist and explorer Xu Fu, tricked the King of the Qin dynasty into sending him on a mission to retrieve the elixir of immortality and eternal youth. He stayed in Japan until all the young people he brought with him became old. Since he brought a hundred craftsmen of five different skills with him, that is why we have these fine blades today.

Starting in the Tang dynasty (618-907) warriors frequently travelled to China and offered these blades as tribute. They were very adept at writing both literature and poetry. Since Xu Fu went to Japan before book burning was done in China Thus a hundred volumes of the *Book of Documents* by Confucius can still be found there. Due to our strict laws, copies of these books cannot be brought over to China. Thus no one in China can read these historical books written in ancient script. Thus the revered book of our elder king (Confucius) can be found in that distant country, but we cannot cross over the great sea to get it. Thinking of these lost books brings tears to my eyes and I find talking about my rusting short sword brings me no relief.

日本刀の歌 *Song of the Japanese Sword*
Tang Shun-zhi 唐順之(1507~1560)

日本刀歌　唐順之

有レ客贈二我日本刀一、
魚鬚作レ靶青糸練、
重々碧海浮渡來、
身上龍文雜二藻行一、
悵然提レ刀起四顧、
白日高々天囘々、
毛髮凜冽生二鶏皮一、
坐失炎蒸日方永、
聞說倭賣初鑄成、
幾藏埋藏擲二深井一、
日淘月煉火氣靈、
一片凝水鬭二清冷一、
持レ此月中斫二桂樹一、
顧兎應レ知避二光景一、
倭夷塗レ刀用二人血一、
至レ今斑黦維能瑩、
精靈長與レ刀相隨、
清霄恍見夷鬼影、
爾來韜韞頗驕黠、
昨夜三關又聞レ警、
錐能將レ此白龍沙一、
奔膽一斬二單于頸一、
古來神物用有レ時、
且向二囊中一試二鞱韜一、

Five hundred years later, at the height of the Wakou pirate raids, Tang Shun-zhi, a soldier and scholar, wrote a poem using the same title.

Song of the Japanese Sword
Tang Shun-zhi

A guest gave me a Japanese sword, the handle of it was covered with the skin of a fish and wrapped with blue thread. It floated across the deep, deep blue sea to here. The blade is covered with a dragon and intertwined with seaweed. Sadly, I raise the blade up, looking at it all over

Held up high the bright light illuminates the heavens. It causes my hair to stand on end and goosebumps to break out. When I sit the humidity is swept way as if the sun still shines.

I heard that when the Japanese barbarians first began molding swords, they would bury them in a deep well for a long time. A sword emerged only after days of quenching and months of forging, like they are battling with water frozen into a sliver of clear ice.

With such a blade you could even cut the mythical tree that grows on the moon, and the rabbit that lives there must surely flee from this glittering blade. The Japanese barbarians paint their Katana with human blood. Those who may face it should be prepared to have their blood splattered across it.

As I hold a blade infused with spiritual energy, I feel as if I am part of it. A flash of light from this blade makes night bright as day and in the blue sky I can see the shadow of the barbarian, and it looks like a devil.

The Tartary nomads that dwell in the north of our country frequently display their arrogance, this night too bells rang out from three gates.

Who will wield this white dragon made of iron and use it to fly up into the sky, and, with one swing, take the head of the supreme leader of the nomads?

I face the sword in its wrapping, a thing that was surely used ancient myths and legends, and begin to draw it forth.

單刀法選
The Japanese Pirate Sword
Selected Katana Techniques

長鎗法選
*Selected Long Spear
Techniques*

蹶張心法
*How to Use the Foot Drawn
Crossbow*

The Author

The Japanese Pirate Sword was written by Cheng Zongyou, who lived 1561-1636. Cheng was the son of a wealthy merchant. Cheng became interested in martial arts from a young age so he decided to study at the Shaolin Temple instead of continuing the family business. Cheng studied at the Shaolin Temple for over ten years and later published several books on martial arts including illustrated guides to the Shaolin staff, spear and unarmed fighting. These were the first documents detailing Shaolin techniques, which had only been orally transmitted up to that point.

The Japanese sword techniques in this book are ones Cheng learned from a man named Liu Yunfeng 劉雲峰. Liu, who is Chinese, is said to have studied directly with Japanese sword practitioners. Given the time period he may well have been a Wakou pirate.

About the Translation

The Japanese Pirate Sword is a translation of the Chinese book 單刀法選 read as *Dandaofa Xuan* in Chinese and *Tanto Hosen* in Japanese. Translated directly the title is *Selected Simple Sword Techniques*. The first two Kanji of the title are 單刀 "simple sword" This is one of several terms used at the time to describe the Japanese Katana, in addition to 長刀 "long sword" and 倭刀 "Japanese sword." In this case "simple" means "single edged" as opposed to the double-edged swords widely used in the Chinese military.

Since the techniques shown use the Japanese Katana, the stances are from Japanese sword fighting and the techniques are the ones used by the Wakou pirates, I chose *The Japanese Pirate Sword* as the title. In addition, the names of the techniques will be as they appear in Japanese. The book was originally published in 1614, however the edition used for this translation is part of a three book series *Skills Beyond Farming* 耕餘剩技 published by Cheng Zongyou in 1621. The books are:

蹶張心法 *How to Use the Foot Drawn Crossbow*
長鎗法選 *Selected Long Spear Techniques*
單刀法選 *The Japanese Pirate Sword (Selected Katana Techniques)*

CHENG ZONGYOU

單刀法選
The Japanese Pirate Sword

程宗猷
By Cheng Zongyou
Published 1614

單刀法選

目錄

一

The Japanese Pirate Sword
Table of Contents

- History of the Katana

- Construction of the Katana

- Illustration of the Katana

- Illustrated Explanation of 23 Katana Techniques

- The Illustrated Continuous Katana Training System

- Description of the Continuous Training System

- Map of the Continuous Katana Training System

- 12 Additional Illustrated Katana Techniques

單刀法選

單刀說

新都程沖斗宗猷著　觀其時瀾

弟伯誠宗信　仲深時通

侯民應萬訂　好禹跡時淶閱

涇礽子順　德正時澤

姪君信儒家校　觀正時滇

浙江侶儷氏施昇平較梓

單刀。以雙手用一刀也。其技擅自倭奴殿煉精堅制罷名
度輕利靶鞘等物各各如法非他方之刀可並且善磨整
光耀射目令人寒心其用法左右跳躍奇詐詭秘人莫能
測故長技每每常敗於刀。余故訪求其法有浙師劉雲峰
者得倭之真傳不吝授余頗盡壺奧時南北皆聞亳州郭

The Japanese Pirate Sword
By Cheng Zongyou
Published in 1614

単刀説
An Explanation of the Katana

The Katana is called the Tanto, Simple Sword, since it has a single blade. The Katana is used with a two-handed grip. These techniques were taken from the Japanese, who excelled at using this sword. The blade is forged hard and it is light and sharp. There are prescribed methods for crafting each part of the sword from the handle to the scabbard. No other sword can compare to this craftsmanship. Further, the glint shining off the finely polished blade pierces the eye, chilling those that face it to the bone.

Use the Katana while jumping from side to side in a secretive and deceptive fashion, meaning an opponent cannot predict your movement. Thus even opponents armed with long weapons will invariably fail when faced with this Katana technique. Therefore I sought to learn these techniques.

A man named Ryu Unho 劉雲峰 "Clouds Around the Peaks," a teacher from Sekkoh 浙江, was able to study this weapon. Ryu had received direct instruction in this weapon from a Japanese instructor. Ryu taught me all aspects of this art, without omission, until I had learned the inner mysteries[2] of the Japanese Katana.

At the time, there was a man named Kaku Gotoh "Five Swords" 郭五刀 from Hakushu 亳州 who was famous both north and south of Sekkoh province. I paid a friendly visit to him. However, when I saw the sword master Kaku's technique and comparted it to the sword master Ryu's technique, I found that Ryu's technique was far more refined and was clearly superior to that of Five Swords'.

---

[2] The author uses Konou 壼奧 to refer to the inner mysteries. The word translates directly as "the bottom of the clay pot" but this can also refer to a hallway within the imperial palace. Therefore someplace strictly guarded.

五刀名。後親訪之。然較之劉。則劉之妙。又勝於郭多矣。良

元受劉刀。有勢有法。而無名。今依勢取像。擬其名。使習者

易於記憶其用法。亦惟以身法為要。儆跳超距。眼快手捷

誘而擊之。驚而取之。心手俱化。膽識不亂。方可言妙。今將

八弩燕用。亦惟選數勢繪圖。直述其理之。可以與鎗敵者

若遇他器。而此圓轉鋒利。制勝又在我矣

單刀式說

古云。快馬輕刀。今以倭刀為式。刀長三尺八寸。靶一尺。則長有五

尺。如執輕刀一言。制不得法。鐵不鍊鋼。輕則僥薄砍下一

刀。刀口偏歪一邊。為能殺人。如要堅硬。則刀必厚。厚必重

非有力者不能用也。故制法惟以刀背要厚。自下至尖漸

漸薄去。兩旁脊線要高起。刀口要薄。此即輕重得宜也。鐵

However, while Ryu "Clouds Around the Peaks" taught me his techniques and methodology, there were no names for anything. Therefore, in this book, I have given names to these techniques according to what they represent. This will make it easier for those learning to remember the techniques.

When using the Katana, the most important thing is how you move your body. You need to make big, nimble jumps, have quick eyes, fast hands and be able to invite the enemy to strike. By then startling him you can gain the upper hand. Your mind, hands, bravery and perception will allow your sword technique to be successful. I have drawn the figures armed with both a crossbow and a Katana. I will show various stances and techniques for defense against an opponent armed with a spear. If you should chance to face other weapons then, by using the same circular movements you can deflect your opponent's sharp spearpoint and achieve victory again.

单刀式说
The Construction of the Katana

There is an old saying, *You need a fast horse and a light sword.* The blade of the Watoh, Japanese Katana, is 3 Shaku and 8 Sun, 122 centimeters. The handle is 1 Shaku and 2 Sun, 38 centimeters, thus the total length is 5 Shaku 160 centimeters.

Trying to make a light sword like this is difficult. If you cannot forge the iron into steel, you cannot make a light sword with a thin blade. However, when you strike something with a thin blade, it can bend causing the blade to lose its ability to kill. If you want greater stability then it is necessary to forge a thicker blade, however that will make the sword heavier. It will require a man of great strength to wield such a blade.

Therefore, the Japanese Katana are thicker on the back of the blade, and taper toward the cutting edge. If the blade is not forged with high ridgelines on either side, the cutting edge cannot be thin. By forging a sword in this manner, you can solve the problem of weight.

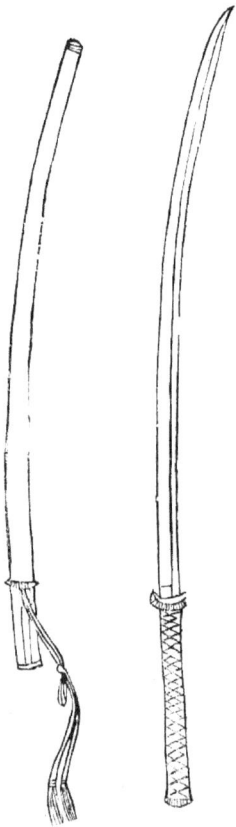

要久煉去渣屎磨時無麻子小黚如鏡一樣光彩則遇潮
汗亦不致上銹乃鐵多煉少是久煉成鋼也刀鞘內要寛
刀口寸金箍入鞘口略緊勿鬆緊鬆亦要得宜以便出入
如用弩帶刀刀長八尺靶長九寸共長三尺七寸不可過
長恐懸帶腰間用弩不便鞘用皮制其法載前用弩蕪鎗

刀說中

單刀式圖

The iron used in these swords must be forged over a long period in order to remove impurities from the metal. Polishing removes even the smallest of pockmarks until the blade shines like a mirror. If any saltwater or sweat gets on the blade it will rust. In other words, the swordsmith spent a great deal of time to carefully craft these blades.

The inside of the scabbard has to be wide. The opening of the scabbard has a metal piece fastened to it. However it should neither be too tight nor too loose. It needs to be just snug enough to make drawing and sheathing easy.

When using a crossbow in conjunction with a sword, the blade should be 2 Shaku 8 Sun and the handle 9 Sun. The total length is 3 Shaku and 7 Sun. If you are wearing a long sword on your belt, the scabbard will make it difficult to use your crossbow. The scabbard is made of leather. My book *The Complete Guide to the Foot Drawn Crossbow* discusses this further.

Illustrations from *The Complete Guide to the Foot Drawn Crossbow*, by Cheng Zongyou.	
Standing with a smaller crossbow used when carrying the Katana	Using a foot-stirrup to draw the Crossbow

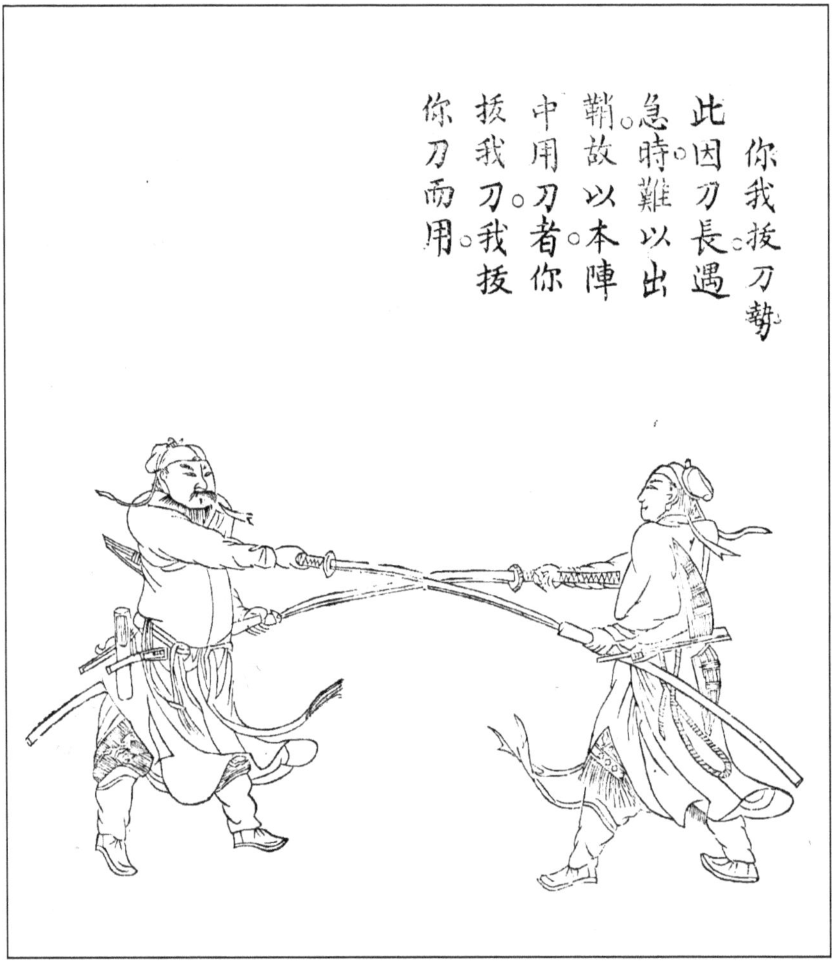
你我拔刀勢。
此因刀長。遇
急時。難以出
鞘。故以本陣
中用刀者。你
拔我刀。我拔
你刀而用。

単刀圖二十三勢
Illustrated Guide to 23 Katana Techniques

1
Ji-ga Batto Sei
How to Draw Each Other's Sword

Since the Katana is long it can be difficult to draw from the scabbard in an emergency. Thus, in our unit, we draw each other's swords. You will draw your partner's Katana and he will draw your Katana.

拔刀出鞘勢

左手持鞘右

手陽持刀靶右

先拔出少許

再用手掌托

挈刀背出離

鞘口以左手

持靶再換右

手共持刀靶

砍殺

2
Batto Shussho Sei
How to Draw Your Sword

Hold the Saya with your left hand, with your right hand on top of your Katana. Your right hand is in Yang, or palm up.[3] Draw your Katana slightly out of its Saya[4]. Hold the back of the blade in the palm of your right hand and draw it all the way out of the Saya. When your Katana is completely free of your Saya, take the handle with your left hand. Then take it with your right hand and position your hands correctly on the handle. With both hands on the handle, you can now cut.

---

3 Yang is part of Yin-Yang, called In-Yo in Japanese. Yin represents the Dark, Moon, Female as well as the left hand. Yang is the Light, Sun and Male as well as the right hand. Further, the palm down is Yin and palm up is Yang.
4 Scabbard

埋頭刃勢

此開左邊門
戶。將左邊身
體向敵餌彼
鎗劄入。以刀
横攔開鎗斜
進右腳換左
手共持靶聽
便砍殺

3
Maitoh Tohsei
Buried Head Sword Technique

You have your left door[5] open. The left side of your body is facing your opponent and you are inviting him to attack you with his spear. The moment he tries to pierce you, use your Katana to block his spear from the side. Step diagonally forward with your right foot and, joining your left hand to the handle, cut down as hard as you can.

---

[5] "Left Door" seems to refer to the left side of your body. This could also be translated as "Left Gate."

入洞刀勢

此亦開左邊
門戶側身欲
空餌彼鎗入
則將刀自下
撩起也鎗進
右步單手自
下斜撥而上

4
Nyudo Tohsei
Entering the Cave Sword Technique

Your left door is open in this stance as well. With your body facing to the side you are indicating you are vulnerable, and inviting the opponent to attack with his spear. If he attacks, then use your Katana to thrust the shaft of his spear up from below. Step forward with you right foot and cut diagonally upward from below holding your sword one-handed.

單撩刀勢

此先或立埋
頭勢或入洞
勢餌彼鎗刣
入我將刀橫
揭起開彼鎗
斜進右脚單
手自下撩起

一刀

5
Tanryoh Tohsei
One-Handed Rising Cut Technique

First of all, stand in either Buried Head Sword Stance or Entering the Cave Sword Stance and invite your opponent to attack with his spear. If he attacks respond by sweeping your sword across the side of his spear, knocking it aside. Then step diagonally forward with your right foot and cut up from below. This should be a cut and lift.

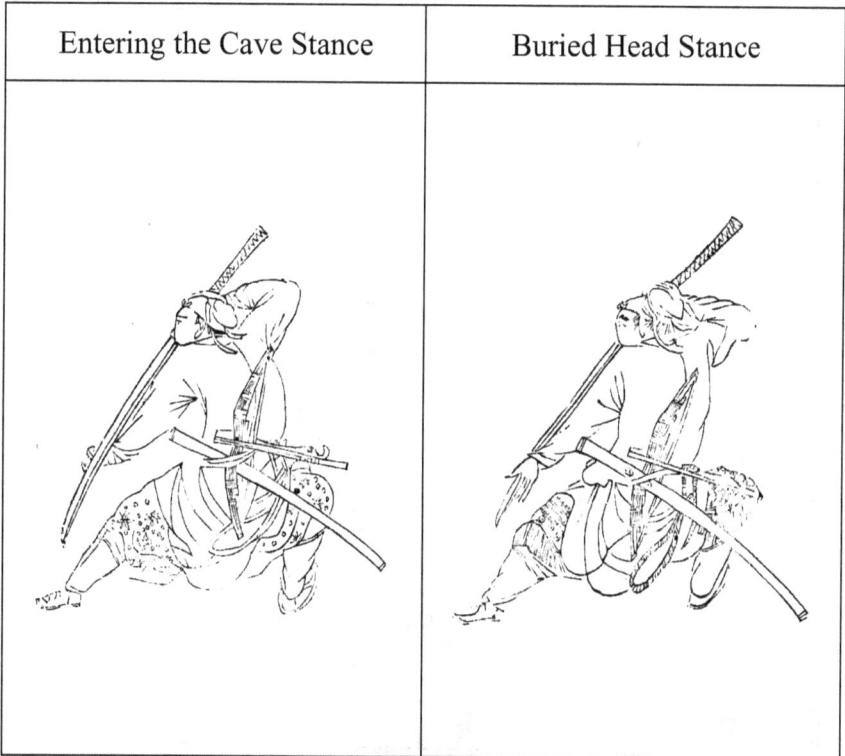

Entering the Cave Stance	Buried Head Stance

腰砍刀勢
此先單手撩
一刀其勢力
巳歸於左邊
單手再復回
橫砍一刀

6
Yohkan Tohsei
Waist Cut Technique

First of all, cut and lift upward one-handed. When your cut is returning to the left, turn this into a one-handed horizontal cut. Use the power from that cut to bring your sword to the left, then cut again with one hand. This time you are cutting across horizontally.

右獨立刀勢

此開右邊門
戶彼鎗劄入。
則將刀往右
後一攬開鎗
斜進右步為
左獨立聽便
砍殺。

7
Migi Dokuritsu Tohsei
Right Single Leg Katana Technique

Open up the door on your right side. When your opponent stabs with his spear, swing your Katana back and to the right, knocking his spear aside.

When you step diagonally forward with your right foot, go into Left Supporting Sword Stance. Then cut down as hard as you can.

左獨立刀勢
此開左邊門
戶彼鎗剳入。
則將刀往左。
後一攪開鎗。
斜進右步砍
一刀。

8
Hidari Dokuritsu Tohsei
Left Single Leg Katana Technique

Open the door on your left side. When your opponent stabs with his spear, cut back and to the left to sweep his spear aside. Step diagonally forward with your right foot and cut down with your Katana.

左提撩刀勢

此亦開右邊

門戶彼鎗刴入自

下斜撩而上

則將刀自

進左步復成

右提撩聽便

砍殺。此二勢乃

技之絕也。

26

9
Hidari Teiryo Tohsei
Left Meet and Lift Katana Technique

Open the door on your right side. If your opponent stabs with his spear, swing your Katana diagonally upward from below, striking and lifting his spear. Step forward with your left foot and you will be in Right Meet and Lift stance. Cut down as hard as you can.

The Japanese excel at these two movements and this technique is very hard to defend against.

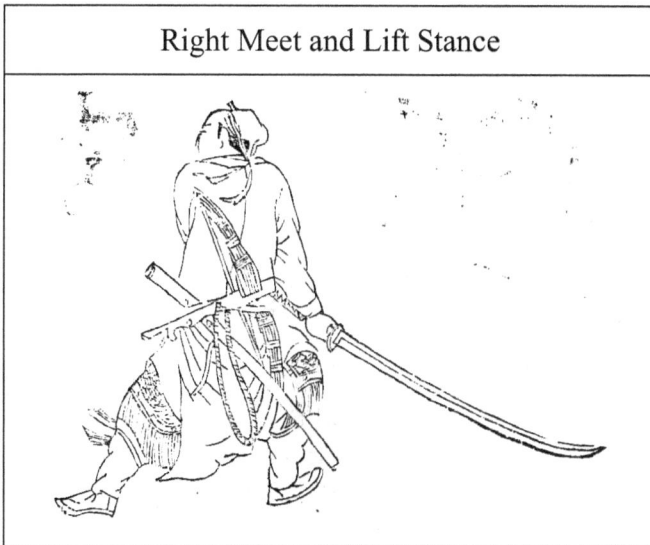

Right Meet and Lift Stance

拗步刀勢

此左腳向前。開右邊門戶。彼鎗往右後。將刀剗入。則一攬進右腳。再進左腳。剪步斜入。聽便砍殺。

10
Yoho Tohsei
Cross-Step Katana Technique

Stand with your left foot forward and the door on your right side open. If your opponent stabs with his spear, swing your Katana to the right and back, knocking his spear away. Step forward with your right foot and then again with your left. Take a short, quick diagonal step toward your opponent and cut down as hard as you can.

低看刀勢

此亦開右邊
門戶彼鎗劄
入則將刀往
右一格進右
安於左邊復
成上弓勢此
二勢左右格
鎗兩邊閃躲。
進步跟鎗勿
離聽便砍殺。

単刀法選

11
Teikan Tohsei
Watching From Below Katana Technique

Open up your right door. If your opponent stabs with his spear, swing your sword to the right one time as you step across your left foot with your right. You are now in Upper Bow stance.

Use these two movements, Watching From Below and Upper Bow, to fend off the opponent's spear. Twist your body first to one side, then to the other, avoiding your opponent's attacks. Advance while keeping the shaft of your opponent's spear close to you and then cut down as hard as you can.

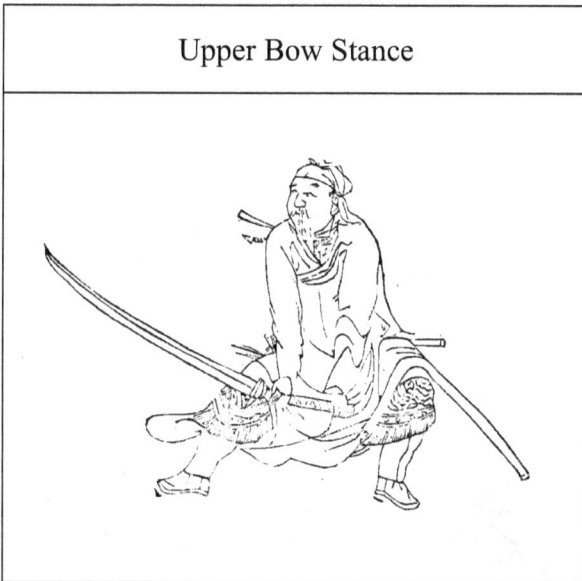

Upper Bow Stance

右提撩刀勢

此亦開左邊
門戶彼鎗劄
入則將刀自
下斜撩而上
進右步則成
左提撩。

12
Migi Teiryo Tohsei
Right Meet and Lift Katana Technique

Open the door on your left side. When your opponent stabs with his spear, swing your Katana diagonally upward from below, striking and lifting his spear.

Step forward with your right foot and you will be in Left Meet and Lift stance.

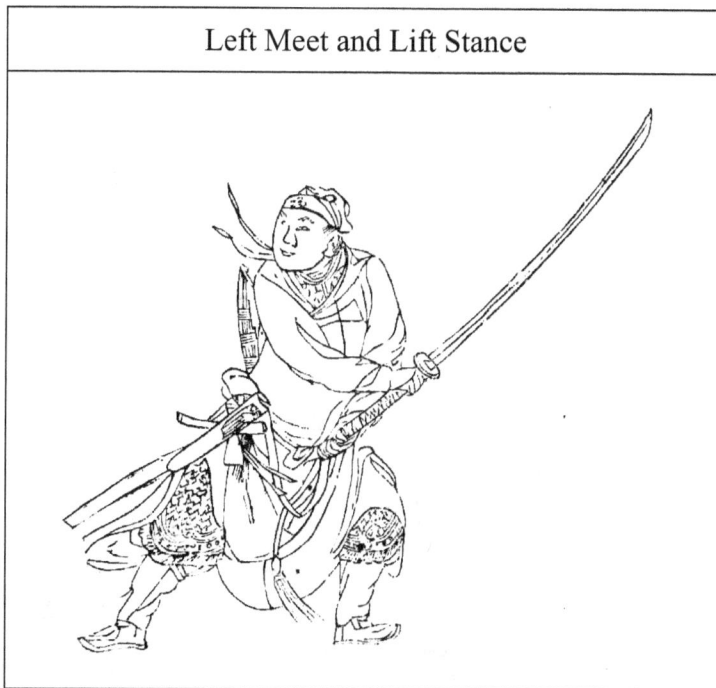

Left Meet and Lift Stance

外看刀势

此開右邊門

戶彼鎗劄入。

我進右腳往右

左用刀往彼鎗進

推開彼腳偷進

左腳右腳偷進

步滾身跳橫進

再進左腳又進

靠一刀又進一

右腳往右一

攬復砍一刀。

13
Gaikan Tohsei
Watching From the Outside Katana Technique

Open the door on your right side. When your opponent stabs with his spear, step diagonally left with your right foot and sweep his spear out to your right. Step forward with your left foot and then step forward with your right in a thief's step, so you are on the ball of your right foot. Leap up like a fountain of water. Step forward with your left foot again. Sweep your Katana to the left then step forward with your right and cut to your right. Finally cut down again.

上弓刀勢

此將刀斜橫
右膝前開當
面門戶彼鎗
剳入則將刀
往左一格進
互步於右邊
則成低看勢。

14
Jokyu Tohsei
Stringing a Bow Sword Stance

Hold your Katana diagonally in front of your right knee. Stand with your front door open. When your opponent stabs with his spear, deflect it to your left with your Katana. Step across to the right with your left foot and you end up in Watching from Below Stance.

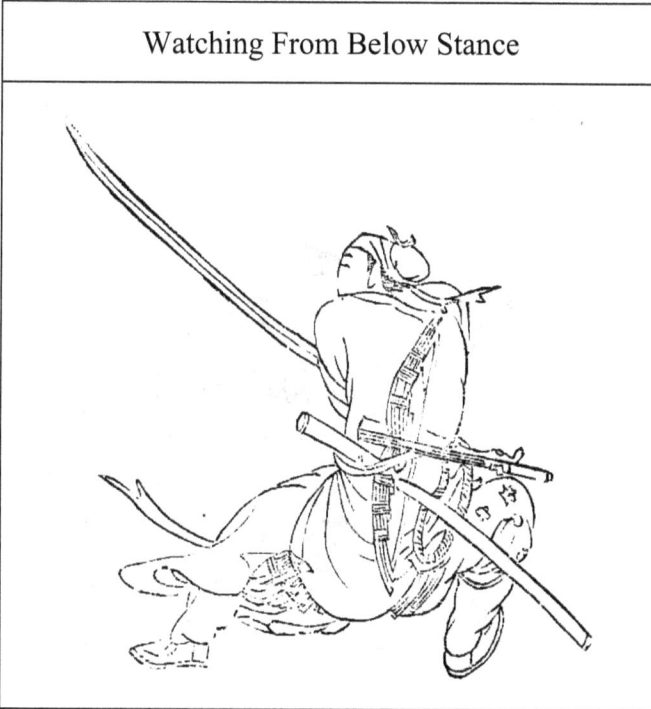

Watching From Below Stance

左定膝刀勢

將刀推出。按
於左膝上。故
鎗即有拏劈。
如鎗左攔開
刀則退左步。
變成上弓勢。
如鎗右拏開
刀將身略後。
一坐變成低
看勢鎗再劄
入聽便砍殺。

15
Hidari Teishitsu Tohsei
Braced on the Left Knee Katana Technique

Place the pommel of your Katana on top of your left knee, with the blade facing forward. When your opponent attacks with a spear thrust, defect it to the side or knock it down. If your opponent's spear thrust forces your Katana to the left, step back with your left foot into Stringing a Bow Stance.

If the impact of the spear on your Katana pushes you to the right, shift your weight back slightly as if you were sitting down. This mean you go into Watching From Below stance. If your opponent thrusts in with his spear again, cut down as hard as you can.

Stringing a Bow Stance	Watching From Below Stance

右定膝刀勢
此將刀推出按
右膝上。如彼左
右劈我。我即那○左
步進。用刀揆削○
彼鎗彼劈我脚。○
用刀一提彼劈○
我面用刀即纔○
彼砍勢彼攔我
外看勢彼攔我
刀即變上弓勢。
聽便砍殺。

單刀法選

16
Migi Teishitsu Tohsei
Braced on the Right Knee Katana Technique

Angle your Katana out in front of you, placing the pommel on the top of your right knee. Step forward the moment the opponent stabs at you with his spear to either the left or right side of your body. Use your Katana to scrape down the shaft of his spear. If he tries to stab your legs, knock the blow downwards. If he stabs to your face, use your Katana to cut down. If your opponent deflects your Katana, shift to Watching From the Outside stance. If he blocks your Katana, shift into Stringing a Bow stance.

Stringing a Bow	Watching From the Outside

朝天刀勢

此以左肩背胯脚
向敵餌彼鎗剳入。
◎我◎懸◎起◎左脚將刀
背往左一攬開鎗。
隨進右脚砍殺。

17
Choten Tohsei
Raised to the Heavens Katana Technique

Your left shoulder as well as your back, thighs and legs should all be facing your opponent, inviting him to stab you with his spear. When he stabs, raise your left leg, sweep down to the left with the back of your Katana, thereby knocking his spear aside. Immediately step forward with your right foot and cut.

迎推刀勢

此先立外看
勢開右邊門
戶彼鎗剿不
實則將刀往
右一推開彼
鎗彼復實剿
我懷裏略偷
左腳於右砍
斷彼鎗。

18
Geisui Tohsei
Draw in and Force Out Katana Technique

First stand in Watching From the Outside Stance, with the door on your right side open. If your opponent does not make a committed attack with his spear, force it forward and to the right with your Katana.

When he commits to a strike with his spear to the center of your chest, with your left foot, step slightly to the right using the thief's step, and cut his spear in half.

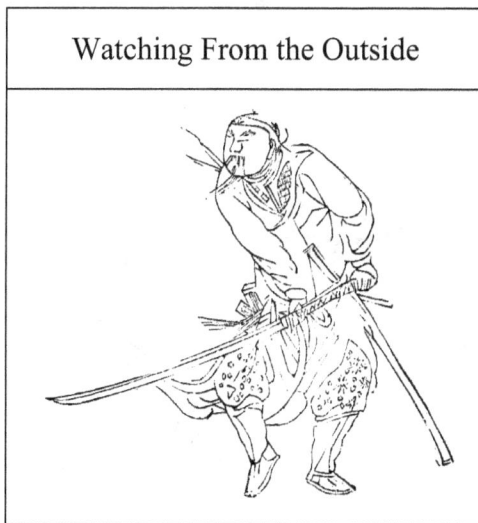

Watching From the Outside

刀背格鐵鈀勢

刀口薄始利。
如遇彼用鐵
了鐵鈀重器
之類。若將刀
口欲格則刀
口必傷。何以
殺敵。故用刀
背以勢中之
法。擊格為妙

19
Tohhai Kaku Tekkisei
Using the Back of your Blade to Block Iron Weapons Technique

The blade of your Katana is sharp because it is thin. If your opponent is attacking with a heavy iron polearm like a trident and you block with the blade, your Katana will invariably become damaged. You will then have trouble killing your opponent.

Thus when you are in such a situation, employ this technique that uses the back of the Katana, you will gradually become adept at the subtleties of Kobo, meaning both offense and defense.

藏刀勢
此因彼鎗變
幻難測故懸
持小刀二三
把用一把藏
挈左手以左
肩背向敵勿
令敵見使之
無防以便將
刀飛刺

20
Zohtohsei
Stored Knife Technique

Your opponent is using his spear in an unpredictable manner, preventing you from being able to clearly see his intent. Therefore you should always have two or three knives ready.

Hold one in your left hand, as covertly as possible. Turn your left shoulder and back towards your opponent, if your opponent does not realize what you have done, it will be easy to throw a knife at him.

飛刀勢

飛刀勢
此將小刀飛
刺去彼必招
架乘此之機
用刀砍入乃
短技長用也。

21
Hitohsei
Flying Katana Technique

When you throw your knife at him, he will invariably move to deflect it. Use that chance to advance and cut with your Katana. In other words this is a quick technique that sets you up for a full attack.

收刀入鞘勢

此先將左手

持刀靶再換

手陽掌托拏

刀背入鞘

22
Shutoh Nyutohsei
How to Sheathe Your Katana

First take the handle of your Katana in your left hand. Next, switch your hand and hold the blade with your right hand in Yang, or palm up. Then slide the Katana into your scabbard.

續總刀圖說

以前刀法著著皆是臨敵實用苟不以成路刀勢習演精
熟則持刀運用進退跳躍環轉之法不盡雖云著著實用
猶恐臨敵掣肘故總列成路刀法一圖而前圖諸勢備載
在中又續刀勢十二圖於後以便習演者觀覽苐習演之
刀當用重長者使臨敵用帶弩之刀則驍快輕利矣然全
刀勢多倘力微者持重刀難以跳舞終局當聽用者力之
長短分為兩節三節習演毋拘定格可也

続総刀圖説
Illustrated Continuous Katana Training System Explanation

Each of the previous Katana methods are practical and can be used against the enemy. However it is not enough just to practice and refine these sword techniques. When using the Katana, advancing, retreating, leaping and turning are insufficient.

It is said, "Each and every move should be practical." Therefore to prevent you from being hindered when facing the enemy I have made a sequence of moves for you to follow. This diagram contains all the previously introduced techniques.

There are also an additional 12 illustrated techniques. You can use these to help in your training. At first, you should practice with a heavy sword. Then also practice while carrying the crossbow. It is quick and light and effective.

There are many techniques in this training sequence. If a person is weak, it may prove difficult to complete the entire set of leaping and dancing with a heavy sword. Thus the practitioner should judge his or her own strength and divide the sequence into two or three sections. You can adjust the method as necessary each time.

Order of Movements for the Training Sequences

總敘單刀一路

北望南用起並足左帶刀勢右轉身出刀勢壓刀勢丟刀

接刀按虎勢進左步入洞勢單撩刀勢單回刀腰砍勢懸

左足左獨立勢攬一刀斜砍懸右足右獨立勢進右步迎

推刺刀勢一刺挽一刀退右步低看勢退左步轉身背二刺漫頭五花

砍勢偷左步攬一刀砍一刀迎推刺刀勢攬一刀砍一刀

左轉身左單擺漫頭五花右轉身右單擺攬一刀砍一刀

迎推刺刀勢三刺東洋牧四上弓勢花翬一刀進左步低

插勢攬一刀進右步砍一刀觌五花單提刀勢左手擦外

鎗進右步單刺刀勢進左步砍五花擔肩勢左手撥裏鎗

進右步砍一刀偷左步斜削勢北望南用終五花迎轉南

望北用起扴步勢偷右步挽一刀低看勢進右步上弓勢

56

Order of Movements for the Training Sequences

槎一刀跳剪步砍 刀名曰奔剪一跳南望北用終 北望

南用起迎轉上弓勢花拏一刀偷左步回砍勢斜削勢攬

天刀勢舉左足擋一刀斜砍二刀外看勢進左步左定膝

勢左提撩勢架起一刀翻身進右步刺一刀北望南用終

南望北用起五花近轉砍一刀外看勢迎轉推刺一刀剪步

背飲勢南望北用終攬一刀砍一刀五花迎轉砍一刀北

望南用起外看勢進左步左提撩勢進右步右提撩勢隨

身五花左右提撩進退勢進右步右提撩勢扯回復砍一

刀名曰提留南望北用終迎轉收刀勢入鞘勢北望南用

大終

57

Illustration of movements and direction for the Training Sequences

Finish

Illustration of movements and direction for the Training Sequences

1.帶刀勢	2. 出刀勢
Face north, use south. Stand with your feet together. Your Katana should be in your belt on your left side. You should be in Katana Sheathed at Your Side Stance.	Turn to your right and do Drawing Your Katana Technique.
3. 壓刀勢	4. 丟刀接刀
After that enter Pressing Down Katana Stance.	Next, throw and catch your Katana.

5. 按虎勢	6. 入洞勢
Shift to Suppressing the Tiger stance and step forward with your left foot.	Next, step forward with your left foot and take Entering the Cave stance,...
7. 單撩刀勢	8. 腰砍勢
...then shift to One-Handed Rising Cut stance. After that, pull your Katana back one-handed.	Next, take Waist Cut stance, lift your left leg and...

9. 左獨立勢	10. 右獨立勢
....then enter Left Single Leg Katana stance. Do a circular block, then cut diagonally downward.	Next, take Right Single Leg Katana Stance, then step forward with your right foot.
11. 迎推刺刀勢	12. 低看勢
Next take Draw in and Force Out stance, stab forward, draw your Katana back and then step back with your right foot. Translator's note: The Kanji "to stab" has been inserted into the name of this stance.	Enter Watching From Below stance, step back with your left foot then turn around to face the enemy.

13. 背砍勢	14. 迎推刺刀勢
Shift your Katana to Back Cut stance, then step with your left foot using thief's step. Do a circular block then cut down.	Shift to Draw in and Force Out stance, stab forward, then cut a five-petaled flower over your head.
15. 左單擺	16. 右單擺
Go into Left Single Leg stance and cut a five-petaled flower over your head, then turn to the right. Translator's Note: "Left Single Leg Stance" as well as the following "Right Single Leg Stance" are likely alternate names.	Go into Right Single Leg stance, do a circular deflection and cut down.

17. 迎推刺刀勢	18. 上弓勢
Shift to Draw in and Force Out stance, attack with three stabs, draw your Katana back as they do in Japan. Then step back with your right foot. Translator's Note: The meaning of Three stabs or Triple stab is unclear. Japan is referred to as "island to the east."	Take Stringing a Bow stance and cut "plucked flower" once, then step forward with your left. Translator's Note: The meaning of "plucked flower" is unclear but it differs from "five-petaled flower."
19. 低插勢	20. 單提刀勢
Switch to Low Push stance and do a circular block. Then step forward with your right foot. Cut down once then rotate the blade overhead in five-petaled flower.	Take One-Handed Lift stance and use your left hand to shove the spear away. Then step forward with your right.

21. 單刺刀勢	22. 擔肩勢
Shift to One-Handed Stab stance, step forward with your left and cut five-petaled flower.	Take One-Handed on the Shoulder and use your left hand to push the spear away. Then step forward with your right and cut down. Then take a thief's step with your left foot.
23. 斜削勢	24. 扣步勢
Take Diagonal Shave stance and Facing North, Attacking South ends. Do a five-petaled flower cut and turn and face the enemy. Now Facing South, Attacking North begins here.	Go into Cross-Step stance and take a thief's step with your right foot. Pull your Katana back.

25. 低看勢	26. 上弓勢
Enter Watching From Below stance and step forward with your right foot.	Then switch to Stringing a Bow Sword Stance. Cut horizontally once, then advance with leaping scissors and cut down. This technique is known as Rapid Scissors Jump. Facing South, Attacking North ends here.
27.上弓勢	28. 回砍勢
Turn around and begin Facing North, Attacking South. Take Stringing a Bow stance cut "plucked flower" once and then take a thief's step with your left.	Take Rotating Cut stance. Translator's Note: This appears to be an alternate name for Back Cut Katana Technique.

29. 斜削勢	30. 朝天刀勢
Then go into Diagonal Shave stance. Do a circular block, then leap off your right foot and cut down with your Katana. Cut horizontally then leap off your left foot and cut down. Leap three times "reversing wave" style and then push into...	...Raised to the Heavens stance. Lift your left foot, do a circular block and cut down diagonally with your Katana.
31. 外看勢	32. 左定膝勢
Then shift to Watching From the Outside stance and step forward with your left foot.	Switch to Braced on the Left Knee stance and...

33. 左提撩勢	34. 外看勢
...transition to Left Meet and Lift stance. Raise the blade while bracing it with your (left) hand. Turn around and step forward with your right foot. Stab forward. This ends Looking North, Attacking South.	Begin Facing South, Attacking North. Do a five-petaled flower turn and face the enemy. Cut down once and take Watching From the Outside stance. Invite in an attack and then push back, stabbing with your Katana. Then scissor step.
35. 背砍勢	36. 外看勢
Transition into Back Cut stance and Facing South, Attacking North ends. Do a circular block, cut down and then do a five-petaled flower turn and face the enemy. Cut down once.	Facing North, Attacking South begins. Take Watching From the Outside stance and step forward with your left.

37. 左提撩勢	38. 右提撩勢
Take Left Meet and Lift stance and step forward with your right foot.	Transition into Right Meet and Lift stance. Turn your body left with a five-petaled flower turn. Take Right Meet and Lift Advance and Retreat stance. Step forward with your right foot.
39. 右提撩勢	40. 收刀入鞘勢
From Right Meet and Lift stance, turn and cut down as hard as you can, recover the blade and cut down again. This is known as Lifting and Stopping. Facing North, Attacking South ends here.	Turn and face the enemy. Sheathe your sword. Final end to Facing North, Attacking South.

帶刀勢

二足並立惟
右膝稍彎左
膝直站名為
雌雄腳坌手
按刀鞘右手
持刀靶以左
肩向前顚步
進左腳於右
再左轉身進
右步出刀

續刀勢圖

続刀勢圖
Illustrated Guide to Katana Techniques
Part 2

1
Tai Tohsei
Katana Sheathed at Your Side Stance

Stand with your feet parallel. Your right knee should be slightly bent, with your left leg extended. This way of standing is known as Male and Female legs.

Your left hand should be on your scabbard and your right hand on the handle. With your left shoulder facing forward, step diagonally forward using a cross-step with your left foot. As you step diagonally right with your left foot, your body will rotate clockwise. Then, as you step with your right foot, draw your Katana.

出刀勢

右手陽掌持靶。出刀於右。斜橫刀尖在左。示胸腹大空。向敵彼鎗劄入。略。偷左脚移於後。用刀靶拶。下鎗。隨加左手共持刀靶。則刀尖斜橫右邊。以右肩向敵。彼鎗又劄入。即起拏砍一刀。如成外看勢。彼鎗又劄入。斜進右脚。用刀背勾開鎗。即進左脚砍殺。○又一着。如前出刀之勢。彼鎗劄入。亦如前殺步將刀靶拶下鎗。大偷左脚右轉身進右步。背砍一刀。

2
Shuttohsei
Drawing Your Katana Technique

Your right hand should be holding the handle in Yang, or palm up. Pull your Katana out diagonally to the right. The point of your Katana should be on your left.

Since you are standing with your chest and stomach wide open, when your opponent stabs with his spear, shift your left foot slightly back, and press the handle of your Katana on the shaft of his spear. Immediately grab the handle of the sword with your left hand. The tip of your Katana should be pointed diagonally to your right side. Your right shoulder is facing your opponent. When he attacks with his spear, knock it up and then cut.

You should end up win a stance like Watching From the Outside. If he attacks with his spear again, step diagonally forward with your right foot. Keep the back of your Katana against his spear, step forward with your left foot and cut.

There is another way to do Drawing Your Katana. When the opponent stabs with his spear, respond as before, pushing down onto the shaft with the handle of your sword. Take a big thief's step with your left foot, standing on the ball of that foot. Then step with your right and cut down.

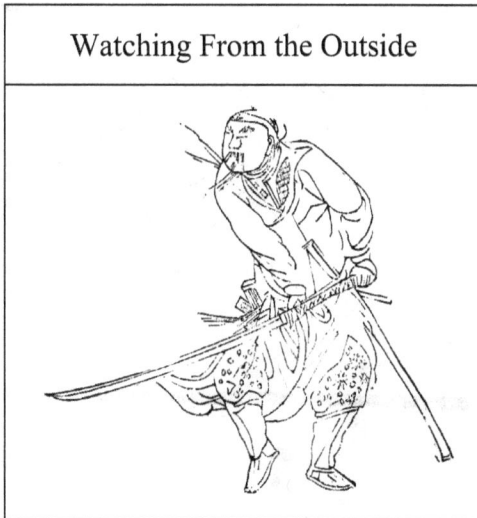

Watching From the Outside

壓刀勢

將右手陰持
刀。蹲身壓下
低勢。左手直
伸於後刀尖
斜向上。以便
丟刀高起。

2
Attohsei
Pressing Katana Technique

Hold your Katana with your right hand in Yin, or palm down. Lean your upper body down so you are in a low stance. Extend your left arm out behind you. The tip of your sword should be angled upwards. This makes it easy to throw your Katana up in the air.

丟刀接刀勢

壓刀將刀口向下丟起刀待
刀落下右手陽仰接刀但刀
丟起落下毋使刀轉動則接
刀待舵刀口向前則便運用
如刀丟起落下轉動不定及
接持刀口不能向前或左或
右則刀難於運用矣

3
Toh Tohsetsu Tohsei
Throwing and Catching Your Katana

You throw your Katana up in the air and wait for it to fall. Catch the Katana in your right hand, which is in Yang, or palm up. Make sure the blade doesn't rotate as it falls. It is best for the blade to be facing forward when you catch the handle. Be aware that if the Katana rotates as it falls, and the blade isn't facing forward when you catch it, you will have trouble transitioning to a left or right cut.

按虎刀勢。
接刀往右手。
即成此勢再
好進步聽變
埋頭入洞二
勢從便砍殺。

5
Anko Tohsei
Suppressing the Tiger Katana Technique

Hold your Katana in your right hand and immediately position your body as shown. As you step forward again shift into either Buried Head or Entering the Cave stance. Then cut down as hard as you can.

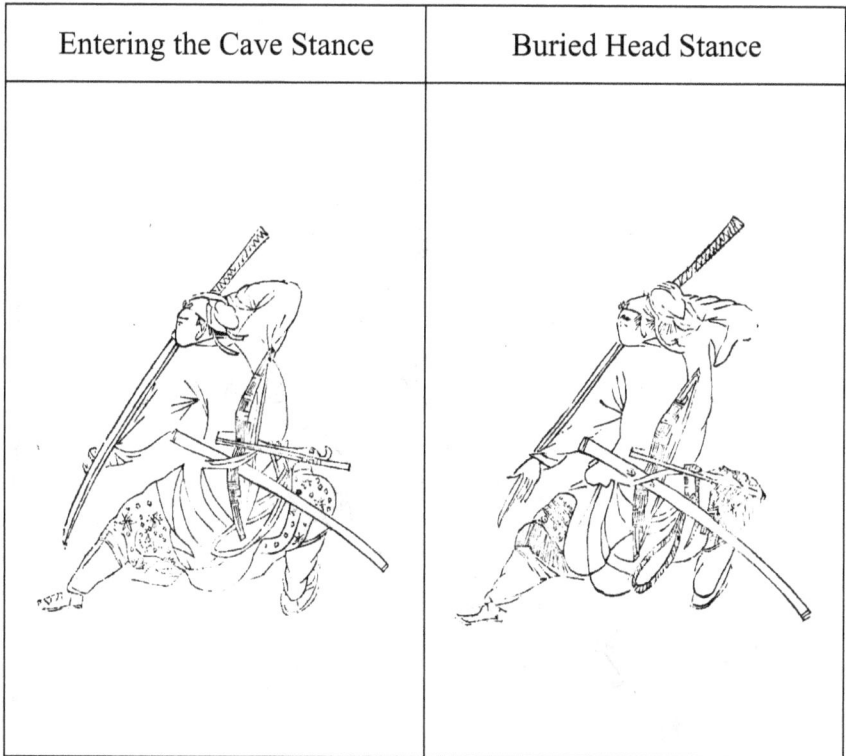

Entering the Cave Stance	Buried Head Stance

背砍刀勢

如先立外看
勢彼鎗從右
劄入我將刀
往右推開鎗
進左脚偷右
步左轉身橫
靠一刀

6
Haikan Tohsei
Back Cut Katana Technique

First position yourself in Watching From the Outside stance. When he stabs to your right side with his spear, use your Katana to sweep it to the right. Step forward with your left using thief's walk, onto the ball of your left foot. Rotate your body to the left and stand with your Katana swept behind you.

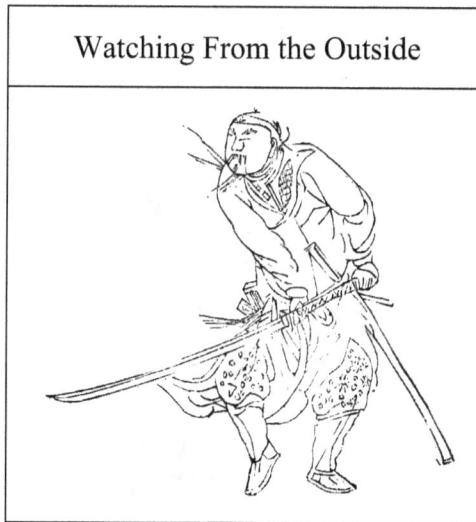

Watching From the Outside

低揷刀勢
先立低看勢。
彼鎗剳左脚。
用低揷一提。
彼鎗起剳面
將刀背勾開。
鎗斜進右脚。
砍殺

82

7
Teisoh Tohsei
Low Push Katana Technique

Begin by going into Watching from Below stance. When your opponent stabs at your left leg with his spear, scoop it up from below with Low Push. When he recovers his spear and stabs at your face, catch it with the back of your Katana, step diagonally forward with your right foot and cut.

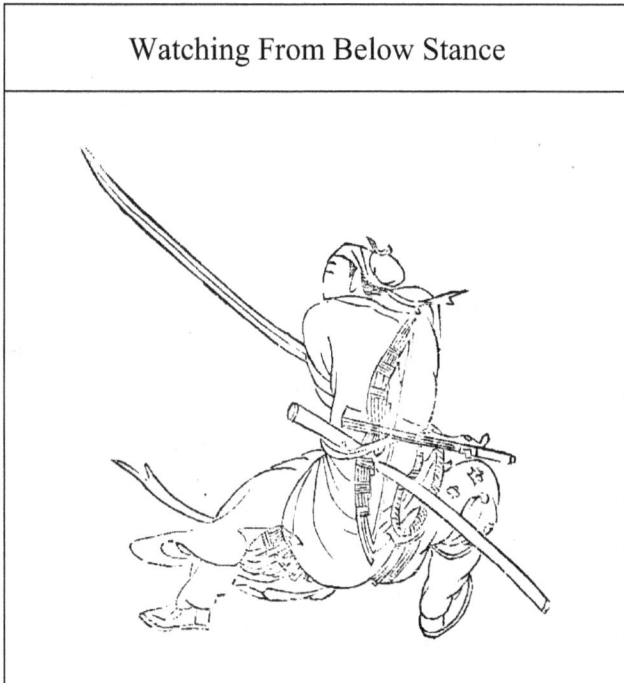

Watching From Below Stance

單提刀勢

右手持刀將左
身併手側偏於右
右邊特露出左
手外腹脇誘彼
鎗劄入斜進左
步於右將左手
挽開鎗隨進右
步單刀平直刺
去。

8
Tantei Tohsei
One-Handed Lift Katana Technique

Hold your Katana in your right hand. Both your body and your right arm should be leaning to the right. Your left hand should be angled out, exposing your ribs and lower stomach, thereby inviting the opponent to stab with his spear. When he stabs, step diagonally to the right with your left foot.

Your left hand makes contact with the shaft of the spear, allowing it to slide across your palm as you force it to the left. At the same time, advance your right leg and with one hand stab forward with your Katana parallel to the ground.

單剝刀勢

單手剌去一
刀收回挽五
花曲左手肘。
墊起刀背徑
頭上過擔於
右肩上。

9
Tanshi Tohsei
One-Handed Stab Katana Technique

Stab forward with your Katana held one-handed. As you draw your sword back swing it around as if you are tracing the shape of a 5 petaled flower. Bend your left elbow, raise the back of the sword towards you on a diagonal. Raise it over your head until the back of the blade is resting on your shoulder.

擔肩刀勢

將刀橫放右肩前
手偏垂於左特露
出左手裡腹脅誘
彼鎗劄入用左肘
往右橫墊開鎗左
右二脚斜跳而入
隨加左手共持刀
靶砍殺

單提擔肩刀勢乃
人見此誘大誘空即欺
多常是用鎗着實
倭奴謂之法但
去常墮計中矣
故云欺敵者七
劄之。

10
Tanken Tohsei
One-Handed on the Shoulder Technique

Stand with the Katana across your right shoulder, with the tip facing forward. Your hand is loose. Your left hand is out to the side so that exposing your armpit and abdomen on your left, inviting your opponent to stab with his spear. When he stabs, use your left elbow to force the shaft of his spear down and to the right, knocking it aside.

Leap diagonally forward two steps, first left then right. Grab the handle of your Katana with your left hand and cut down.

This One-Handed on the Shoulder technique is used by the Japanese. It is a trick to draw their opponent in. More than a few people have looked with contempt at Japanese standing this way, with their arms splayed out everywhere. This stance caused many soldiers to commit fully to their thrusts and, thinking they had an easy kill, completely forgot everything but their attack. This is just like the saying goes, *mocking an opponent can lead to your death.*

斜削刀勢
如抱刀懷中⑪
以右肩向敵。
彼劄右脚。用
刀斜削開鎗
則刀偏於右。
覺彼起鎗劄
面偷左步將
刀遠開鎗順
砍一刀。

11
Shasaku Tohsei
Diagonal Shave Katana Technique

With your right shoulder facing your opponent, hold your Katana up against your chest as if you are cradling it. When the opponent stabs at your right leg, slice upward into the shaft, forcing it aside. In other words, you have moved so your Katana is under your right armpit. Your opponent recovers his spear and then stabs to your face.

Respond by stepping forward with your left foot using thief's step, meaning on the ball of your foot. Block the spear but allow it to pass by before cutting down.

收刀勢

用完刀法將
刀往頭上左
遶一刀曲彎
右手以刀背
閣在肘上再
用手反挈刀
靶入鞘。

12
Shutohsei
How to Sheathe Your Katana

When you have finished this Toho, or sword sequence, hold the Katana over your head and rotate it counter-clockwise. Bend your right elbow so the back of the blade rests on your elbow.

Then switch your hand around and sheathe it in your scabbard.[6]

---

[6] The historian Kasao Kyoji made the following comments regarding these techniques in his 2019 book *Overview of Chinese Martial Arts History* 増訂 中国武術史大観,

As the note on #10 indicates, these 12 methods were not formulated by Cheng Zongyou. Further, though there are some elaborate flourishes, overall these 12 stances follow the fundamentals of the previous 22 techniques and clearly they are Tojutsu (Kenjutsu) techniques that originate from Japanese schools.

Beginning in the Edo Era the theory and methodology of Japanese Kenjutsu became more refined, thereby losing the original wild and savage elements. By looking at The Japanese Pirate Sword we can catch a glimpse at the original source of what became premodern Japanese Kenjutsu, and appreciate its vitality.

以上鎗刀用法雖以粗語直述各勢之中盖余皆演棍法

勢圖皆以歌訣述之雖便觀者記憶而變幻之意猶未能

詳悉故今粗述鎗刀法誠欲人之易曉也然有心妙者尚

不必定拘愚見但目視敵如何殺來手中運鎗刀如何格

去身體如何左右躲閃脚步如何進退等法至於心手俱

化隨機而應惟以順勢順力為妙如逆之則不能稱矣

也歷云十八般武藝惟鎗稱王諸器皆用鎗法比試欲制

其長與疾也故余刀法亦以鎗法諭之如遇各器觀其體

當知其用以各勢中用法破之無有不勝者譬虎惟猛有

牙爪之利鬬必以牙爪傷人牛力巨有角之利鬬必以角

觸人能在此中解悟類推可稱因敵制勝矣及此何以謂

技哉。

This ends my book on how to use the Katana against a spear. I wrote this book in coarse language (the vernacular/ everyday language) and I have described each technique in a straightforward manner. My readers no doubt recall some of the same techniques as in my book *The Illustrated Guide to the Kon Staff.*

Most of these techniques are described using poems. However, though recording information in lines of poetry makes it easier for the practitioner to remember, details of how each move is done can be forgotten. Thus, I have used coarse language to describe these Katana versus spear techniques because I sincerely desire people to understand them clearly.

Certainly those who are already adept need not concern themselves with my humble opinion. However, watch the enemy. How does he seek to kill you? Though you have a sword or a spear in your hands, how will you defend? Which way will you dodge to avoid his attack? Left or right? How will you move your feet? Will you advance or will you retreat? The mind and body should be unified and ready to react should a chance present itself.

You should move according to the techniques and add power, subtlety, where appropriate. Failing to do this will mean you fail at your goal.

History tells us that there are 18 Martial Arts, but the spear is known as the "King of Weapons." All the other weapons are tested against the spear method. They seek to control the spear's long reach and speed. This is why this Katana method is taught in conjunction with the spear.

Anytime you encounter another kind of weapon observe its form and how it is employed and consider what technique you would use to defeat it. By doing this you will never know defeat. For example, a fierce male tiger has claws and teeth. Surely it will use them when fighting to injure a person. Oxen are powerful and they have horns they can use. In a fight they will always use them to gore a person.

Consider the following analogy, "adapt to the enemy in order to win." If you are not doing this, why speak of Waza?

www.ingramcontent.com/pod-product-compliance
Lightning Source LLC
Chambersburg PA
CBHW052040270326
41931CB00012B/2573